Hard Labor

Hilarious REAL-LIFE stories about the things men and women do during pregnancy ～ From conception to that first dirty diaper!

Written, compiled and illustrated by
Brian Krueger and Jack York

Cincinnati, Ohio

Published in Cincinnati, Ohio by Armchair Press, 3616 White Oak Drive, Suite 2,
Cincinnati, Ohio 45247, (513) 741-8666, fax (513) 281-0214.

For book trade orders contact Login Publishers Consortium, 1436 West Randolph Street,
Chicago, Illinois 60607, (800) 626-4330, fax (312) 733-3107.

For gift trade orders contact Sourcebooks, Inc., 121 North Washington, Suite 2,
Naperville, Illinois 60540, (800) 727-8866, fax (708) 961-2168.

Library of Congress Catalog Card Number 94-71191
ISBN 0-9634739-3-X

Printed in the United States of America
First Printing October 1994

10 9 8 7 6 5 4 3 2 1

Dedicated to our Moms:
Julia Krueger and Joan York

Two wonderful ladies who have endured a combined
total of twelve Hard Labors. Thanks for grinning and
bearing us — we hope we were worth the pain.

Love,
Joel and Brian

Thanks to you...

...this book is possible. We've enjoyed hearing your stories and greatly appreciate your allowing us to come into your homes, offices and hospitals to create this book. We sincerely thank:

John Adler, M.D. for his wonderful insights, humorous anecdotes and persistent efforts in helping us get these stories. Thanks also to his wife Diana for welcoming us and an entourage of doctors into their home.

Alliea Phipps, Robert Strub, M.D., Lynnie Hartley and Karl Ziesmann, M.D. for letting us hang out with your outstanding doctors, nurses and medical professionals.

Good Samaritan Hospital, The Christ Hospital, Bethesda North Hospital and Bethesda Oak Hospital for opening your doors to us.

Most of all thanks to the many people across America who shared their stories with us:

Pamela Rosenacker, Ray Thomas, Arthur Jones, Theresa Pickett, Jim Smith, Linda Morris, Steve Liuzza, Patsie Voight, Zeke Zschiedrich, Bobby Gunther, Bill Walters, Lisa Merker, Jim Buddington, Becky Starling, Jerry Bloom, Mark Horm, Linda Fanter, Charlotte Meyers, Lori Bowden, Jay Self, Phyllis Penn, Naomi Fletcher, Dan Schottenstein, Leah Grubbs, Betty Rogers, John Dengel, Ed McDougle, Dee Phillips, John Wagner, Debbie Smikoski, Kevin McCandless, Joe Rozanski, Chris Emmons, Phyllis Smith, Steve Hart, Michael Pearson, Margaret Craig, Marcelle Lloyd, Paul Grasso, Tom Romeo, Arlene Eggleton, Bill Knight, Debbie Reynolds, David LeMoine, Mark Nuar, Charlie Lawlor, Rene Reynolds, Keith Johnson, Brian Slazer, Chris Marantino, Debra Lake, Linda Wyatt, Joanne Rollind, Virginia Luck, Harvey Hill, William Willis, June Naples, George Honchar, Dave Mann, Gayland Sabey, Wendy Durtschi, Kathy Taylor, Lisa Lewis, Peggy Kenney, Kathy McVey, Tina Feuer, Darbie Pierce, Denise Carter, Linda Kurlas, Ken and Amy Bushman, Sandy DeWitt, Tanya and Mike McMahon, Leonard Kuehnle, Susan and Gary Waits, Grace and Joe, Walt and Judy Harrell, Samantha Harrell, Thomas and Mary Ann Edwards, Betty and Don Rickards, Mike and Chris McElroy, Marilyn Mathis, Denise Breengate, Bob Brown, Mike Bolland,

Thanks To You... (continued)

Pam Frank, Joan Sattler, Randy Gomez, Mary Jo Beziat, Joan Turner, Anne Deem, David and Beth Callahan, Diane and Larry Siereveld, Daniel Deady, Bob and Barb Eviston, Eric Stamler, Joe Caligaris, Kevin Fitzgerald, Betsy and Sherif Awadalla, Walt Bowers, Molly Johnson, Claudia Gruber, Frank Froehlich, Bob Stephens, Elbert Nelson, Adam and Natalie Adler, Mary Pat Burke, Kristin Spradlin, Nancy Mulcahey, Julie Stalf, Cheryl Miller, Lois Dronberger, Debbie Engel, Carol Mastin, Juanita Barnes, Joy Murray, Lisa Schloemer, Timothy A. Tate, Edna Burns, Mary Stevie, Lynn Orme, Lisa Hill, Nelda Sturgill, Jane Ferone, Sue Ellen Jacobs, Debi Johnson, Stephanie Jones, Sue Hudgins, Cindy Lachet, Shirley Wilson, Janie Johnson, Elvena Ayres, Ron Sanzone, Lana Elliot, Jon Fackler, Bob Jacobs, Kathy Kleinhold, Navkaran Singh, Don Aichholz, Cyd Abner, Gina York, Bob and Debbie Shaw, John and Jackie Merritt, Mark Mahoney, Jenny York, Guy and Allison York, Marty Gillaspy, Graham Spencer, Dennis Gray, Joan and Jack York, Bob and Julia Krueger, Julie York, Mike and Mary Murray, Janie and Doug Lyons, Jim Krueger, Joe and Julie Schneider, Jenny Krueger, Jackie and Ed Evers, Tom LaFary, Steve and Sue LaFary, Jill LaFary, Bob and Carol York, Andy and Suzanne Hauck, Dick and Kathy Zeinner, Bill and Jean Hoelker, Paul Krueger, Sean Morphew, Judy and Dave Thomas, Diane Jones, Joi Thomas, Jamie and Don Beresch, Bill Krueger, Anne York, Sean O'Toole, Len and Carolyn Stahl, Cliff and Martha York, Barb and Joe Schaffer, Jerry and Robin Schaffer, Jan Schmid, Jill Hoelker,

Jim and Patty Hoelker, Jeff and Caren Hoelker, Joe and Louise Hoelker, Bryan and Jodie Humpert, Jim and Michele Powers, Video Grayphics, Jesse Abner, Sandy and Jerry Bedacht, Scott and Carla Reiman, Tom and Lisa Bedacht, Ken and Gayle Bushman, Bill and Carol McCauley, Anne McBreen, Nancy and Erik Bloemendaal, Dave and Mary Hils, Cheryl Rountree, Linda Kump, Marysue Wright, Barbara Hauber, Joe and Shannon Gabar, Mary Kay Gerst, Peggy Flanagan, Suzanne and Jim Finke, Mark and Monica Purcell, Kristi McBreen, Joe and Valerie Herdman, Bonnie Schwecke, Deborah Kocis, Leslie Thomas, Joanne Hausman, Deena Parsons, Julia Smith, John Mitravich, Jo Anne Robinson, Terri Dunyak, Frank E. Scudder, Jr., Wendy and Cam Bommer, Tim and Anne Shaffer, Paul and Sylvia Halley-Safar, Jane Rottmueller, Ginny Konerman, Susan Horwarth, Wendy Fern Weisberg, Lisa Maertz, Julie Nagel, Joyce Horn, Beth Clark, Julie Piller, Blake and Kathleen Gettys, Vickie Morgan, Nadine Young, Wendy Yurchak, Meg Fledderman, Kevin Morgan, Gary and Evelyn Kirschner, Judi Boersma, Ginger Murphy, Tom and Julie Clyde, Susan Neal, Mollie McCandless, Vince Lombardi, Dan and Claudia Hawkins, Tracey Casey, Lori Wiebell, Joan Appelbaum, Mick and Peggy Besse, Valerie Wilke, Monica Rettig, Steve Schmuelling, Pam and Joe Schoenlaub, Mike and Lynn Honold, Rita and Steve Bushman, Holly and Rob Hursong, Amy and Chuck Scott and to all those anonymous folks who sent their questionnaires back.

Contents

Prescription for Laughter

Foreward by John D. Adler, M.D.

Delivering babies has been the main source of pleasure and fulfillment in my professional life. Obstetrics remains as the "happy" field of medicine. To watch a newborn infant gasp its first breath and utter its first cry renews the spirit as no other human event can.

However, until a healthy baby is born and the mother is safely removed from harm, tension overwhelms everyone involved. Relieving this tension with humor has always been a mainstay of obstetrics. This book shows the range of humor that having a baby inspires. Jack and Brian have gathered these stories from me and a host of other healthcare professionals, as well as from thousands of couples across America. Hilarious stories about conception, pregnancy and delivery-room antics abound in this easily readable format. You can enjoy this book while planning your family or even reminiscing about your own child-bearing experiences.

Perhaps amidst the laughter and good feelings this book engenders, you may be reminded just how special it is to bring a new life into the world. The wonder and renewal are contagious.

John D. Adler, M.D.
President, Mt. Auburn Obstetrics & Gynecologic Associates, Inc.
Cincinnati, Ohio

From The Armchair To The Maternity Ward – And Back!

Yeah, yeah, yeah, we know...What could two men who have absolutely no experience or credentials possibly know about pregnancy?

Well, for starters, we went on a nationwide, 14,500-mile, 26-city journey listening to more than 7,000 people complain about their mates. Astounded by the many hilarious stories we heard about pregnancy, we felt we had no other choice but to go where few men dared go before us – into the maternity ward!

Jumping feet-first into the world of pregnancy required sending surveys nationwide; conducting hundreds of personal interviews with doctors, nurses, midwives and couples; and spending countless hours in maternity wards observing actual births first-hand. We wore 45-pound empathy bellies, took ipecac to simulate morning sickness and participated in mock deliveries – stirrups and all!

With research almost complete, we sat in the lounge of the maternity ward at The Christ Hospital in Cincinnati, Ohio, proudly exclaiming, "Yes, we the 'Armchair Experts,' really know exactly what it's like to be pregnant!"

Then it happened.

At precisely 2:31 p.m. EST on June 22, 1994, we heard a scream so piercing, so chilling it brought a dead silence to the room. With fists clenched and eyes wide open we nervously asked, "What was that?" In a curiously casual manner a nurse replied, "Oh, it's probably the lady who's going natural. The head must have just come out."

At that moment we knew. No matter what we did, no matter how many people we talked to, no matter how many contraptions we wore, the real pain and fulfillment of childbearing would always elude us.

So it is with humble respect that we dedicate this book to mothers, the true pregnancy experts. We hope these real-life stories about raging hormones, bulging bodies, neurotic husbands, pain-crazed patients and amused obstetricians will have you laughing in the stirrups.

Yeah, yeah, yeah, we know...We'll never know what it's really like to be pregnant. But at least we're trying.

The stories you
are about to read
are all true!

Rotund Romance

"When you're seven months pregnant you don't feel too romantic. Hoping to get that feeling back, I cooked a nice dinner followed by a very romantic movie. I left the room during the movie to change into my sexy, two-piece negligee. Well, it sure didn't look the same as it did last August. Instead of the top covering my waist, it barely came down to my navel, with a big belly hanging out. It was kind of embarrassing, but we both got a good laugh."

Hard Labor

McLabor

"My husband actually went through the drive-thru at *McDonald's* on the way to the hospital when I was in labor with our first child."

Other Things Men Have Done While Wife Was In Labor

- Went on week-long fishing trip
- Drove through a car wash
- Had to wait for pizza delivery man
- Finished watching *Dukes of Hazard*
- Waited until he batted in a softball game
- Test drove his new bulldozer
- Watched the end of the *Indy Time Trials*
- Had to clean plaster dust out of new house

Tee Time

"My labor schedule unfortunately conflicted with my husband's tee time. He dropped me off at the hospital on his way to the golf course and called me from the ninth hole on his cellular phone. I told him we had a healthy baby boy. He said, 'Wow, this is a great day. I got a birdie on the sixth.'"

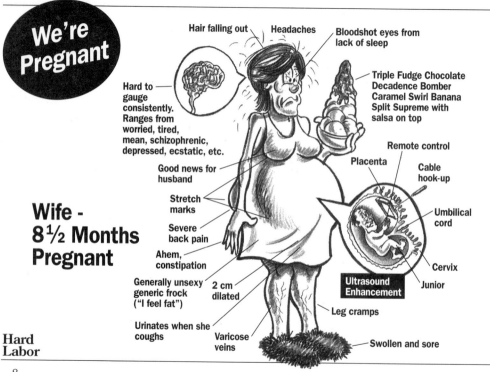

We're Pregnant

Hair falling out

Headaches

Bloodshot eyes from lack of sleep

Triple Fudge Chocolate Decadence Bomber Caramel Swirl Banana Split Supreme with salsa on top

Hard to gauge consistently. Ranges from worried, tired, mean, schizophrenic, depressed, ecstatic, etc.

Good news for husband

Stretch marks

Severe back pain

Ahem, constipation

Generally unsexy generic frock ("I feel fat")

2 cm dilated

Urinates when she coughs

Varicose veins

Remote control

Placenta

Cable hook-up

Umbilical cord

Cervix

Junior

Ultrasound Enhancement

Leg cramps

Swollen and sore

Wife - 8½ Months Pregnant

Hard Labor

8

Husband - All The Time

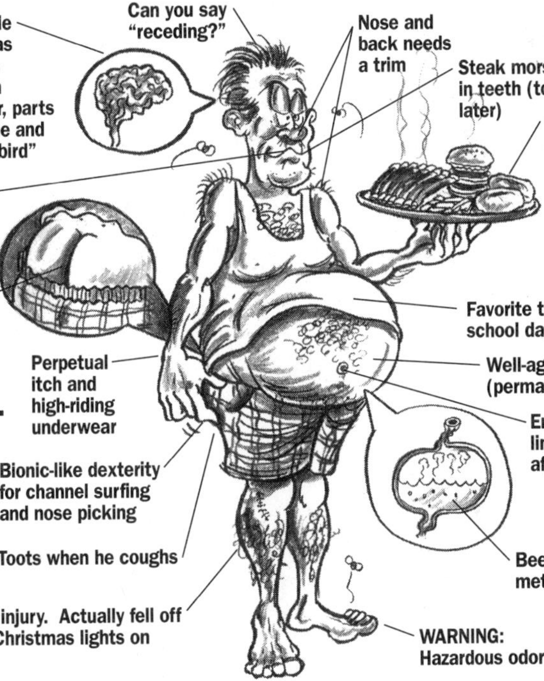

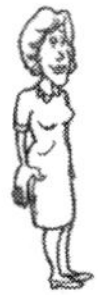

Around the House

"A woman in the early stages of labor called our hospital to ask the doctor what to do. The doctor told her to walk around the house for awhile and call him back. A couple of hours later, the woman's husband called the doctor and said, 'Doc, can we come in yet? We've been walking around the house for two hours and it's ten degrees outside, very dark, and my wife is freezing.'"

Hard Labor

Cave Cork

"My wife had the brilliant idea of going spelunking (cave exploring) when she was eight months pregnant. She ended up getting stuck in a crevice and I had to call the fire department to come and pull her out."

Bug Off!

"I totally missed the birth of our new son. On the way to the hospital I felt pretty guilty, so I decided to pick some flowers out of our neighbors' yard to give to my wife. When I gave her the flowers, a parade of red ants crawled out and went all over her body!"

The Pregnancy Test

Women's #1 complaint about men is that they don't help enough around the house. During pregnancy, this can really put your relationship to the test. With your wife carrying around an extra 45 pounds, not to mention a multitude of other physical ailments, this is your opportunity to make some major brownie points. This is the ideal time for all you men out there to put down your remote controls, get your duffs out of the *La-Z-Boy* and do your fair share.

To help you get started, we offer these household hints which were given to us by real fathers who passed the test:

Hard
Labor

Hint #1 "Instead of cleaning potatoes one at a time under the faucet, you can put a 20lb. bag in the washing machine all at once."

Hint #2 "Never dust under anything. How could dust possibly get under something?"

Hint #3 "Use the 'smell test' to determine if clothes are *really* dirty. Sometimes they can be worn a few more times."

Hint #4 "If the baby has a dirty diaper, you can use that hose on the kitchen sink to spray its butt off, but you better clean the sink out good."

Hard
Labor

Hint #5 "Bath towels never need to be washed. They don't get dirty because you're clean when you dry yourself off with them."

Hint #6 "I packed a week's worth of dishes in the back of my pickup truck and drove it through a car wash. It worked pretty good, but I wouldn't use the high pressure sprayer, because it breaks the dishes."

Jeep Trick

"My wife was two weeks late with the baby, so I took her four-wheeling on railroad tracks to try to induce labor."

Eli Kirschner & his mom Evelyn.

Beetle Mania

"Years ago, *Volkswagen* offered $100 to anyone who gave birth in the *VW Bug*. When I was in labor, my husband drove me around town for about seven hours hoping the baby would come. By then, I was fed up. I grabbed him by the throat and snarled, 'Get me to the hospital – NOW!' "

**Hard
Labor**

Not Just for Breakfast Anymore

"During all three of my pregnancies, I had a fear that my water would break while I was in the grocery store. So every time I went shopping I made a bee-line for the juice aisle. I carried a jar of apple juice the entire time I shopped so if my water happened to break I could drop the juice and exit the store in a hurry!"

Hard Labor

WARNING
TO EXPECTANT FATHERS

We're only going to say this once. Women have two kinds of bad moods:

1. The **Pregnancy Bad Mood** (replaces PMS during gestation period).

2. The **Husband Did Something Boneheaded Bad Mood.**

Unlike us men, women do not differentiate between the two. To them, every bad mood is a "Husband Did Something Boneheaded Bad Mood." The surest way to incite her wrath is to blame her mood swings on the pregnancy. Any feeble attempts you make to sensitize yourself to this emotional pendulum will only exacerbate the problem. So take our advice: Any time you see that piercing stare, say, **"Honey, I'm sorry, I am a bonehead."**

Hard
Labor

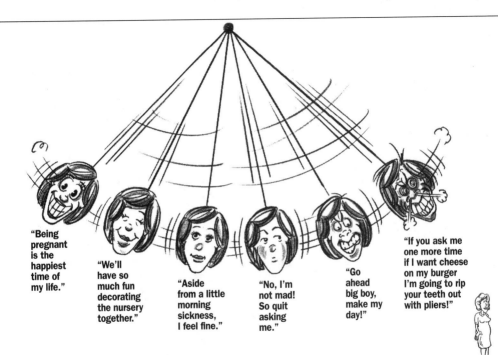

27

Belly Whoppers

"At prenatal water exercise class, fifteen of us pregnant women with our big chests were exercising in the water. In the hot tub next to the pool, four men sat there staring at us with their tongues hanging out.

You could see their shock and disappointment
when all us women got out of the pool
with our big bellies
and bulging
behinds. Serves
them right."

House Call

"My wife went into labor while I was out of town. She was afraid to drive herself to the hospital because she just failed her driving test for the fourth time, but decided to go anyway. On the way, her car swerved off the road, down a hill and through the living room wall of someone's house. She was okay, and the people called the paramedics who picked her up and brought her to the hospital for the delivery of our baby girl."

Hard Labor

Self-Basting Surprise

"As a fertility specialist, I am amazed at the lengths people will go to get pregnant. I heard a story of a lady who got pregnant by inseminating herself with a turkey baster."

Blooming Idiot

"I had been through eighteen hours of labor with my husband at my side when I delivered our first baby. Saying how exhausted *he* was, my husband went home to sleep. The next morning he brought a big bouquet of flowers into the hospital room. I was so touched. He then walked over to the nurse and gave her the flowers, thanking her for all her hard work."

What's In It For You?

For the Wife

License to eat, yell, cry, cuss, nag, sleep, shop, whine and yell again and blame it all on your pregnancy.

For The Husband

Wife's breasts are larger.

Designated driver for the next 9 months.

Mammary Glad

"A pregnant patient of mine was so enthralled with the size of her breasts that she actually weighed them. She came into my office and said, 'Can you believe it, they weigh nine pounds apiece?!'"

Mom TV

"A few weeks after our baby was born I received a call from our local video store. They asked me if I could please come pick up my 'private video.' We had rented the *Cosby* baby video, but by mistake my husband returned the video of the birth of our baby. Another family rented the *Cosby* video only to see me in all my glory. They were shocked and I was quite embarrassed."

Gut-O-Lantern

"Last Halloween I was eight months pregnant. My husband and I were invited to a Halloween party and I needed ideas on what costume to wear. My artist husband suggested going as a witch and painting my stomach like a Jack-O-Lantern. I reluctantly agreed and ended up walking around all night with my big, bare, orange belly exposed and acted like I was carrying a pumpkin. We were the hit of the party."

Hard Labor

43

Bouncing Belly

"During my wife's first pregnancy she gained 33 pounds. One night, while at a high school basketball game, one of the players threw the ball out the gym door. A little boy whispered to my wife, 'If they don't find the ball, can they have the one under your shirt?' "

45

Kids Told Us...

"Mommy, when is her extension cord coming off?"

Three-year-old watching mom breast feed her new brother:
"Mommy, when I feed my baby I'm going to have one chocolate milk booby and one orange juice booby."

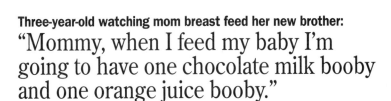

Hard Labor

Teacher:
"What does your dad do?"
Third Grader:
"He drives a truck."
Teacher:
"I thought he was a doctor."
Third Grader:
"No he's not. He delivers babies!"

"My mom has a baby in her belly and it kicked her bellybutton out."

Mr. Organization

"My husband had to have every detail of my delivery planned out exactly. He had a map of three alternative routes, parking locations, hospital floor plans, etc. We did a mock delivery timed with a stopwatch. He gave me computer lists of what to pack, things we learned in childbirth class and his detailed schedule for the next two months. I had to laugh when, as I went into labor, he realized he locked his keys in the car."

Hard Labor

Back to Back

"During a very long and difficult labor with my second child, I asked my husband if he could please rub my back. He said, 'Honey, I've been working in the yard all day, and there is no way your back can possibly hurt as bad as mine.' He then asked me to rub his back."

First Come, First Served

"I was in the waiting room with another man while both our wives were in labor. After only twenty minutes the doctor came out and told me I had a new son. The other man went nuts. He started screaming at the nurses, 'I want to talk to the manager! I've been here for four hours and he's only been here twenty minutes. He got his baby first. Where's my baby?'"

Hard Labor

What If Men Could Get Pregnant?

The Ultimate "What If..." Imagine, if you will, the broad-sweeping impact on every facet of our lives if men could get pregnant. "Real Men" would now be measured by their girth instead of their worth. A new social structure would evolve as our nation's institutions are frantically overhauled. Imagine the changes in:

Sports...
Major League Baseball revises strike zone

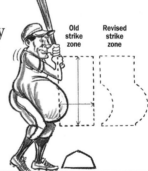

Old strike zone

Revised strike zone

Hard Labor

Hollywood... Schwarzenegger sets new box office records. Stallone wins Oscar for "Mombo."

What If Men Could Get Pregnant? (continued)

Cars...
Big Three automakers announce major
engineering changes to make cars more
pregnancy-friendly.

Government...
Congress revises Family Leave Act, extending
paid maternity leave from 12 weeks to 2 years. Six dissenting
female congresswomen exclaim, "What a bunch of wimps!"

Medicine...
Natural childbirth outlawed. Obstetrics Hall of Fame established.

Jobs...
Morning sickness paralyzes nation's work force. Absentee rate
skyrockets to all-time high of 73%.

Hard
Labor

Sex...
A new breed of sexy men emerges. Fashion and fragrance industries changed forever. Chubby-Whale-Dancers send women into a frenzy.

School's Out

"I've never been so embarrassed in my whole life. While I was teaching my third grade class, my water broke and went all over the floor. They thought I wet my pants."

Remotely Concerned

"When I was in labor, my husband was watching the *NCAA* basketball finals. Unfortunately, the epidural they gave me didn't take, and I was screaming at the top of my lungs. Instead of helping me, my husband put a pillow over my face and turned the volume up on the TV with the remote control."

**Hard
Labor**

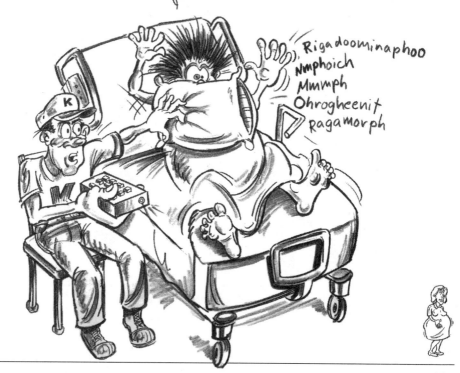

World Serious

"It was during the fifth inning of the 1990 *World Series* that *Cincinnati Reds* pitcher Tom Browning's wife Debbie went into labor. Tom rushed out of the dugout and drove her to the hospital, reserving a seat for himself in the waiting room to watch the rest of the game. With Debbie minutes away from delivery, the baseball game entered the bottom of the ninth in a tie. Thinking Tom might be needed to pitch if the game went into extra innings, manager Lou Pinella appealed to the radio and TV announcers to ask Tom to come back. As Tom watched from the waiting room, *CBS* broadcaster Tim McCarver made the plea on national TV. Tom proved to be the smartest man alive when he elected to stay by his wife's side for the birth of their third child, Tucker."

(The *Reds* ended up winning the game and the *World Series*.)

Engraved in Stone

"Instead of getting a book, like normal people do, to help decide the name of our baby, my husband insisted on going to the local cemetery to look for names on the gravestones."

The Name Game

What To Name The Baby

Case Study: Bud and Sarah Wilson

If it's a boy...		If it's a girl...	
Her ideas	**His ideas**	**Her ideas**	**His ideas**
Zachary	Bud, Jr.	Brittany	Budelia
Jonathan		Ashley	
Shawn		Caitlin	
Tyler		Lindsey	
Blake		Shawna	
Kyle		Whitney	
Cody		Morgan	
Joshua		Tiffany	
Chad		Paige	
Jordan		Amanda	

Hard Labor

Real Names Given To Babies

Nosmo King
Wild Child
Heaven Leigh Joy
Porsche Mercedes
Crystal Shanda Lear
Happy Harvest Fields
Jedidiah Douglas Animal
Big Mike
Lovely Bone
Celery
April Schauer
Semaj (James backwards)
Harley Davidson
Sy Phyllis
Seth Poole

Pat Smear
Lake Cumberland
Mister Dijon
King Solomon
Diamond Sparkle

Twins

Orangello and Lemongello
    (after orange and lemon *Jell-O*)
Boya and Boyb (Boy A and Boy B)
Female and Tamale
Ken and Kenny (Dad was Kenneth)

(These are all actual names found on birth certificates.)

Slippery When Wet

"I was assisting in the delivery of twins, which were coming real fast. The doctor told me to hurry and get suction bulbs to clear their throats. As I ran back into the delivery room, I slipped on the amniotic fluid, doing a head-first, 'Pete Rose' belly flop across the floor. I slid past the doctor and

Sip
Swooosh

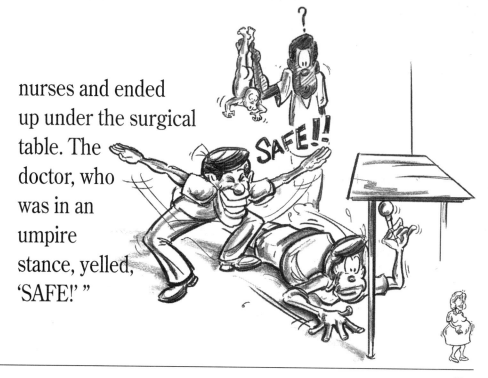

nurses and ended up under the surgical table. The doctor, who was in an umpire stance, yelled, 'SAFE!' "

Two for One

"A major fistfight broke out in one of our delivery rooms when two men showed up, both claiming to be the father."

One for Two

"Talk about a major dilemma. I remember one man who got two women pregnant. Both were in labor at our hospital at the same time and their rooms were next to each other. He didn't know which way to go as they both screamed for help."

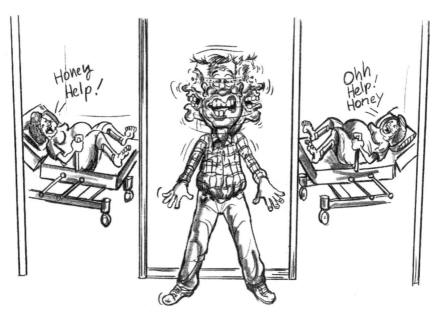

Baby Bookie

"My husband brought six of his friends into the delivery room, and they started a betting pool on when I would deliver, how big the baby would be and whether it would be a boy or a girl. They were screaming and cheering in the delivery room!"

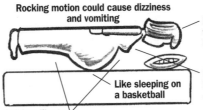

Sleeping 101

Directions for Sleeping When You're Pregnant

Wrong Way #1
Mt. Everest
Technique

Pressure on bladder causes multiple trips to the bathroom

Husband can't see TV over belly

Women never sleep on their backs anyway

Undo stress on back

Wrong Way #2
Teeter-Totter
Technique

Rocking motion could cause dizziness and vomiting

Probable neckaches from holding head in air

Requires gymnastics-like dismount to get out of bed

Like sleeping on a basketball

Children like to play hide-and-seek in voids under body

Hard
Labor

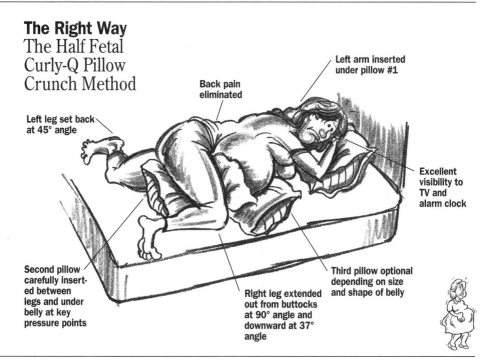

The Right Way
The Half Fetal
Curly-Q Pillow
Crunch Method

Left arm inserted
under pillow #1

Back pain
eliminated

Left leg set back
at 45° angle

Excellent
visibility to
TV and
alarm clock

Second pillow
carefully insert-
ed between
legs and under
belly at key
pressure points

Right leg extended
out from buttocks
at 90° angle and
downward at 37°
angle

Third pillow optional
depending on size
and shape of belly

Sweet Dreams

"When I was pregnant with our first daughter, I always had the strangest dreams. One particular dream was about the birth. Only instead of a baby, I gave birth to a dozen donuts. They kept coming – two or three sets of 'twins' – two bran muffins, two jelly donuts, etc. I remember asking the doctor when they would start breathing."

Hard Labor

Who's on First?

"As a father of four kids, I kind of feel like an expert on fathers in the waiting room. You can tell by their nervousness which baby they're on."

Hard Labor

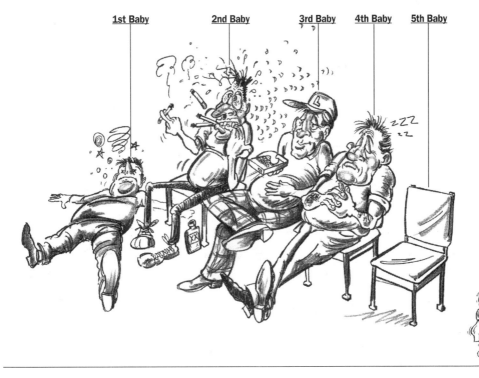

Labor Day Loser

"I'm in hard labor waiting for my high school football coach husband to get home from a championship game. At 11 p.m. he walks in the door, along with a crabby mood, after losing by one point. As I stood with my suitcase, ready to go to the hospital, he barks, 'Could you please have a little compassion here? I just lost a big game by one point and I still haven't had dinner yet.'"

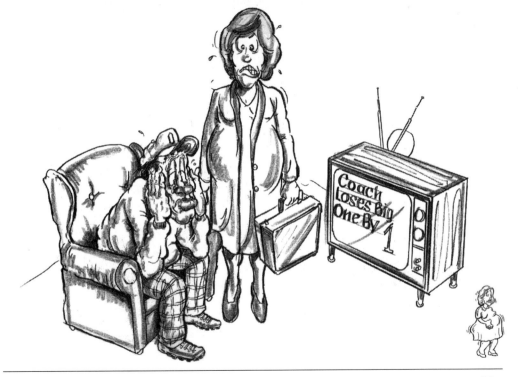

The Omen

"I am one of the authors of this book, and my wife is expecting our first child. I had a dream that we had a baby boy who looked just like me. Right after he came out, he walked to the refrigerator, got a beer and began cussing and screaming at me. He said he wouldn't take any of my crap and that he could do whatever he damn well pleased. I was actually afraid of the little monster."

An Amazing Thing We Learned

Some women develop a habit known as pica when they're pregnant. This causes them to crave, and even eat rather peculiar substances like:

Wood

Hard Labor

Clay

Dirt

Starch

Ashes

Chalk

Drinking Buddy

"During the early months of my pregnancy, I had to be hospitalized for severe morning sickness. My husband brought a cooler of beer and pork rinds to the hospital and sat by my bed feeding his face. The smell made me so sick I thought I was going to die."

Hard Labor

Circum-Decision

"As a nurse, I have to get both parents' approval before their son can be circumcised. When I asked one mother if she wanted her son circumcised, she was unsure and told me to ask her husband. When I asked her husband, he said he wasn't sure either. I then asked him if *he* was circumcised, thinking this would help him decide. He replied, 'You know, it was so long ago, I just don't remember.'"

Hard Labor

Maternity Mooner

"My husband was in the delivery room to watch the birth of our baby. The nurses asked him to put on a hospital gown. When he came out of the bathroom, all he had on was the hospital gown and his old torn-up underwear. The nurses and I were laughing hysterically as he walked around the room with his butt hanging out."

Hard Labor

Birdies, Bogeys and Babies

"As I was putting on the sixteenth green, my pregnant wife, who was driving the cart, went into hard labor. As it turned out, I helped deliver our daughter right there on the sixteenth hole.

Hard Labor

The golf course jokingly sent us an invoice for two additional greens fees."

EASTSIDE GOLF COURSE

INVOICE

BIRTH ON 16th HOLE
GREENS FEE ... $40.00

PAYABLE ON RECEIPT

Say What?

Top Ten Dumbest Things Said During Pregnancy

#10 "Doctor, I think I'm pregnant. I missed my last administration."

#9 Woman when told it was time to have her baby:
"I can't have the baby today. My baby shower is this weekend!"

#8 Dad after hearing doctor ask for large circumcision tool:
"Like father, like son."

Hard Labor

#7 "If I go to a rock concert will my baby go deaf?"

#6 Woman going to get an induction: "I'm here to be seduced."

#5 "Please doctor, give me an epidoodle!"

#4 Husband to doctor after seeing his new daughter:
"Why aren't her ears pierced?"

#3 "I can't believe I'm pregnant! My husband used a condominium."

#2 Doctor to patient: "Are you sexually active?"
Patient: "No, I pretty much just lay there."

And the dumbest thing said during pregnancy was:

#1 "How did I get pregnant?"

Eating for Two

"The worst thing about delivering a baby is that all you can eat is ice chips. While I'm lying there eating ice chips, my husband is pigging out on pizza, submarines, ice cream and pretty much everything else I love to eat."

Rat Patrol

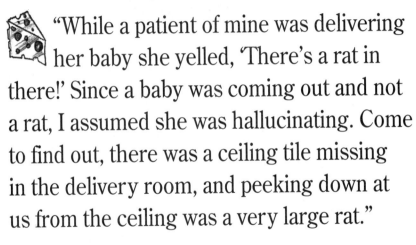 "While a patient of mine was delivering her baby she yelled, 'There's a rat in there!' Since a baby was coming out and not a rat, I assumed she was hallucinating. Come to find out, there was a ceiling tile missing in the delivery room, and peeking down at us from the ceiling was a very large rat."

L'amazing

"My husband was all psyched up for the birth of our first baby. He wore coaching shorts, cleats and a 'University of Lamaze' sweatshirt to the delivery room. He immediately passed out when I got my epidural.

Hard Labor

After being carried out to the waiting room, he had to explain to the other fathers where the University of Lamaze was and what sport he coached."

Gas Can't

"I was two weeks overdue with my third child. I went into labor at 3 a.m. Thinking he would have planned ahead, I asked my husband to get the car ready. He said, 'Um, I think we're out of gas, but don't worry I've got an idea.' He got the lawnmower out, sucked on a hose and siphoned gas out of it. He swallowed gas and started getting nauseous. I gave him ipecac and ended up driving myself to the hospital, stopping along the way so he could vomit."

Hard Labor

Saab Story

"My water broke and went all over the leather seats of my husband's brand new Saab. When we got to the hospital, the nurses put me in a wheelchair and rushed me to the delivery room. My husband didn't even come with us. He just stood there by his car whimpering, 'My poor Saab.'"

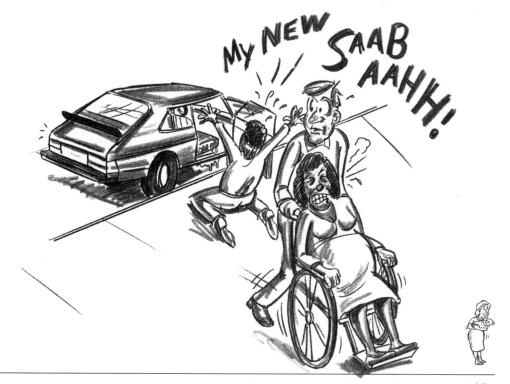

A Fractured Tale

"My wife's water broke and went all over the kitchen floor. As I panicked to get her to the hospital, I slipped in the water and broke my leg. I felt like a dork having to share a room with her at the hospital."

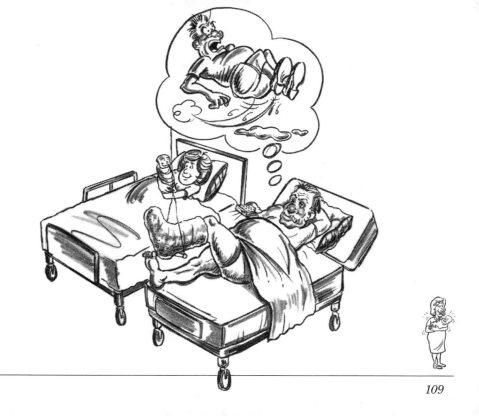

Parking Violation

"My husband took me to the hospital when I was in labor and drove past the entrance and up to the eleventh floor of the parking garage. He told me I needed the exercise."

Clear and Present Danger

"In preparation for delivery, one of our patients was lying on her side with her bare behind to the window. Next thing we knew, a window washer was working his way across the window. He almost fell off the scaffolding when he saw her exposed butt. We were laughing hysterically as we rushed to close the curtains."

Hard Labor

Bright Ideas

Inventions We'd Like To See

For women: It's the pregnancy "Pain Emulator." Now your husband can *really* feel your pain.

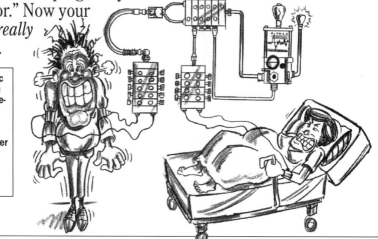

This digital pneumatic and/or hydraulic pain emulator has a double-action adjustable pump, digital valve support bracket and can accurately transfer a relatively equitable amount of pain to receiver (97.634% pain transference)

Hard Labor

For men: Introducing the "Babe-E-Sitter 2000." One push of a button and your baby self-maintenance program begins.

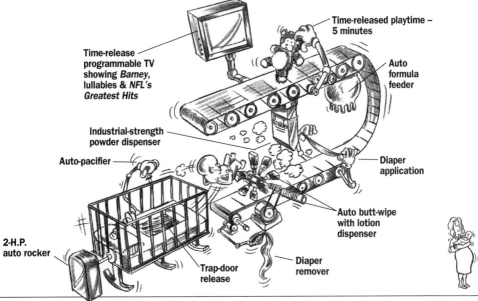

Time-release programmable TV showing *Barney*, lullabies & *NFL's Greatest Hits*

Time-released playtime – 5 minutes

Auto formula feeder

Industrial-strength powder dispenser

Auto-pacifier

Diaper application

Auto butt-wipe with lotion dispenser

2-H.P. auto rocker

Trap-door release

Diaper remover

Exsqueeze Me

"After convincing my wife to 'go natural,' I stood by her side during our daughter's birth. Her excruciating pain during labor caused her to accidentally grab my crotch and squeeze real hard. I felt like I was the one needing the epidural."

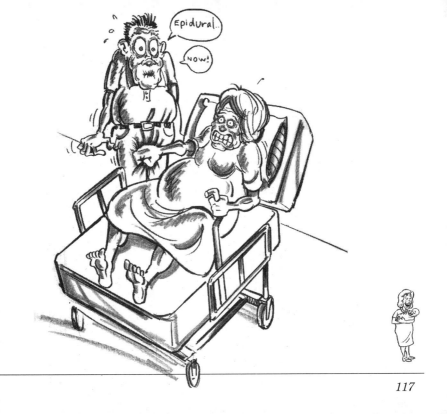

The Full Nelson

"A woman in labor was out of control. When the doctor checked to see if the baby was coming, she got him into a head-lock between her legs. The doctor fell to his knees gasping for air as we nurses fell to the floor laughing."

Hard Labor

Kung Fool

"My husband (who happened to love John Belushi, by the way) dressed up like a Samurai and talked our doctor into letting him cut the cord with a samurai sword."

Hard Labor

Backdraft

"My 'macho man' fireman husband was intent on videotaping our baby's birth. After seeing him turn white and lose his balance, the nurses asked him to sit down. He kept saying, 'Don't worry, I'm a fireman, I've seen it all!' Just as he started to lose it, the nurse grabbed the video camera and filmed him passing out cold, still mumbling, 'But I'm a fireman.' "

That Was Then, This Is Now

Why's grandpa laughing his butt off?
Because in his days it was easy to be a father. All he had to do was take care of business in the bedroom, show up to bring the wife and kid home and pass out cigars to his buddies at the Moose Lodge.

But Not Anymore.
Pregnancy is much more complex today. We fathers are now expected to master the teachings of Ferdinand Lamaze, Bradley and Grantly Dick-Read. We're required to attend childbirth classes, change diapers, do midnight feedings, help pick out color schemes

Hard Labor

for the nursery (even though we think all blue colors match) and know the differences between layettes, bassinets, onesies, bumper guards, breast pumps, mobiles and porta-cribs.

We need to know the perils of second-hand smoke, VDT's, sugar substitutes, caffeine, X-rays, toxic cleaners, food additives, PCB's, nitrates, MSG, radiation, leaded paint, microwaves and hot tubs – not to mention the family cat.

Meanwhile, grandma is fuming.

In her day, when it was time to deliver, she'd go out and grab a pole, squat down and deliver the baby and be back in time to cook a twelve-course dinner.

The scariest thing today's mothers have to encounter is grandma coming in the delivery room and saying, "Well, well, well, there certainly wasn't a place like this when I was in labor. You young kids just don't seem to understand that this is supposed to hurt. Young lady, when I was your age..."

(And life goes on.)

Oh Girl, It's A Boy!

"After having three girls, my husband was praying for a boy the fourth time around. Fathers weren't allowed in the delivery room back then. So when our *son* was born, I told the doctor to wrap him in a pink blanket and put bows in his hair. You could see the disappointment in my husband's eyes when he saw the baby, but he acted happy anyway.

After I lifted the blanket,
he ran around the
hospital yelling,
'Yes, yes, yes,
I got a boy!' "

The Bushman Family

Go Figure

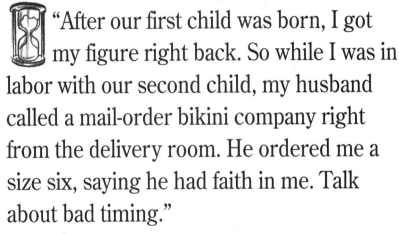 "After our first child was born, I got my figure right back. So while I was in labor with our second child, my husband called a mail-order bikini company right from the delivery room. He ordered me a size six, saying he had faith in me. Talk about bad timing."

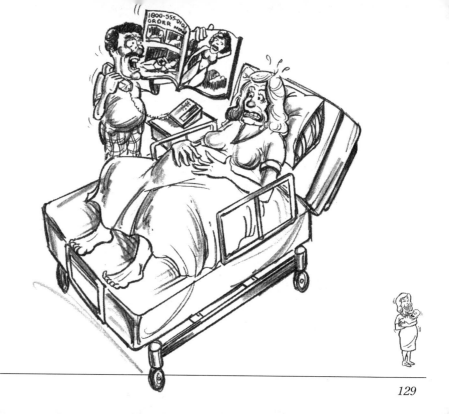

129

Desperate and Dateless

"Some arrogant man asked me out on a date as I admired my newborn twins through the observation window at the hospital nursery."

Hard Labor

Bobbing Baby

"The first time my husband watched our new little girl on his own, he placed her into her swing. When I got home she was still rocking. I took her out of the swing and her head was still moving in a 'swing-like' manner. I asked him how long she had been in the swing. He said, 'Oh...about four hours.'"

Hard Labor

What you think your baby looks like...

What everyone else thinks your baby looks like...

Winston Churchill

E.T.

Top Secret

"When I told a father in the waiting room that his wife had just delivered healthy twin boys, he said, 'That's great, but please don't tell my wife – I want to surprise her.'"

Chip off the Block

"I remember delivering a child that we used to call an FLK – short for 'funny looking kid.' The father couldn't be there for the delivery, but he was on his way. Just as we wondered if this baby was of this planet, the father came charging through the door. Then we realized that the kid looked just like the father. Both had a real long neck, narrow lips, large ears and a pin head."

Hard Labor

Father and Mudder

"In all my years as an obstetrician, the craziest thing I've ever seen came from a big, burley, slow-talking Texan. As I started to deliver his wife's baby, he began throwing mud on the delivery area. I said, 'What in the h--- are you doing? This is a sterile field!' He replied, 'Sir, my grandpappy, my pappy and myself were all born on Texas soil, and I'll be doggoned if this boy ain't gonna do the same!' "

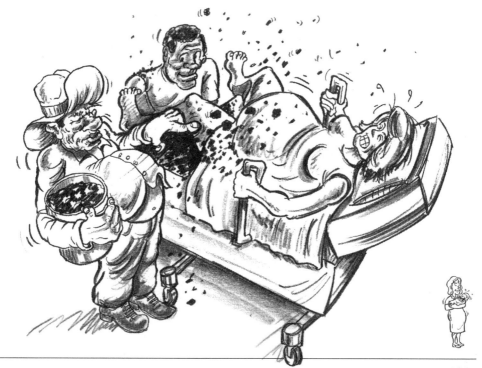

Would you like to be in our next book?

It's easy! All you have to do is send us your funny real-life stories. Include stories on: pregnancy; gripes about your mate; unique marriage engagements; wedding mishaps or funny things kids say and do. You can mail it, fax it or even call it in. And the best part is that your name will be included in our next book. You might even be asked to appear with us on national television to share your story.

All you need to do is fill out the questionnaire on the facing page.

Send to: **Armchair Press**
3616 White Oak Drive, Suite 2
Cincinnati, Ohio 45247
Or fax to: (513) 281-0214
Or call: (513) 741-8666

Name _____

Address _____

Phone _____ Age _____ No. of kids _____

☐ Yes ☐ No   I would like my name included in your next book

☐ Yes ☐ No   I am interested in appearing with you on national
                     television to tell my story

Please write your story here (feel free to use additional paper if necessary) ____

_____

_____

_____

_____

_____

Don't forget our first book!
*Beyond Putting the Toilet Seat Down – 423 real
comments from men and women about their relationships.*

Who are the "Armchair

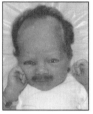 

Brian Krueger

Born and raised in Cincinnati, Ohio, Brian is the second oldest in a family of nine kids. It was on a Tuesday night in 1958 that his mom's water broke during *The Red Skelton Show* (thereby explaining his offbeat sense of humor). Shortly thereafter, Brian arrived, and by his dad's account looked "like a dead chicken."

His passion for art was cultivated in grade school where he was a major doodler, promoted to "class cartoonist" by his high school years. He went on to get a degree in fine arts from Indiana State University and is now an award-winning illustrator whose works have appeared in *Rolling Stone*, on album covers and gallery walls, as well as in the pages of this book.

In his spare time, Brian takes great pleasure in being a professional slob and arguing politics with his longtime girlfriend, Cyd.

Experts" anyway?

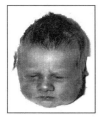 

Jack York

Jack was born and raised in Cincinnati, Ohio, and is the oldest of four kids. Never one to miss a meal, he must have smelled the food when he caused his mom to go into hard labor in a grocery store in 1960. The next day he was born with what his dad called "the biggest head I'd ever seen."

After receiving his undergraduate and graduate degrees in business from the University of Tennessee and the University of Wisconsin, he started to climb the corporate ladder at the consulting firm Arthur D. Little, Inc. When informed that shorts and a ballcap weren't part of the dress code, he politely excused himself from corporate life to begin his entrepreneurial pursuits. He now spends his days in a combination basement, laundry room, weight room, office and shower stall, appropriately attired in his shorts and ballcap.

Married in 1992, he and his wife Gina hope to be telling Hard Labor stories of their own as they are now expecting their first child.

The End